C000046353

THE KEY TO
GUILT-FREE SUCCESS
FOR **WORKING MOMS**

THE KEY TO
GUILT-FREE
SUCCESS FOR
WORKING MOMS

Lose the Stress,
Embrace Your Supermom Powers

ABY MAMBOLEO

WITH TANY SOUSSANA

MAMBOLEO MEDIA GROUP

NEW YORK

Copyright © 2023 Aby Mamboleo, JD/MBA

Published by Mamboleo Media Group

No part of this book may be reproduced, or stored in a retrieval system, or transmitted in any form or by any means, electronic, mechanical, photocopying, recording, or otherwise, without express written permission of the publisher.

https://www.abymamboleo.com

ISBN (paperback): 979-8-218-04010-9
ISBN (ebook): 979-8-218-04011-6

Cover and book design by John Lotte

Manufactured in the U.S.A.

CONTENTS

Introduction—Moving Forward   xi

PART 1   MOMMY/WIFEY HAT

   1   Wake-Up Calls   3

   2   Family First   11

   3   Breakfast on the Run   18

PART 2   ENTREPRENEUR HAT

   4   Escape to the Office   27

   5   Guilt-Ridden at Work   35

   6   Daily Family Multi-Tasking   43

   7   Martial Arts Me-Time   53

PART 3   I'M HOME HAT

   8   Fast Food Dinner Guilt   63

   9   The Children Run the Show   71

  10   Life Goes On   79

This book is dedicated to all
working moms—the superwomen who are the true
Mothers of Multi-tasking. I hear you and I am at
one with you!

For the woman who is evermore stretched in directions
that are beyond manageable, this life we signed up for
is just part of our mommy/wifey package deal.
It is now up to us to make it ALL work.

I'm talking about staying ahead of the "circus"
(aka, drama-du-jour) in the Working Mama Sisterhood.

None of us are alone as we dash around wearing
our superhero hats and dealing with frazzled,
unhinged nerves.

Through the madness, and our cups completely
running over, not all superheroes wear capes.

No, we ladies with full plates have our special
(hard) hats—*and you best believe those Hero hats sparkle.*

Every day, we open our eyes and pull on our "Call Me
a Hero" hats. It's all just part of our daily balancing and
juggling act. *(Okay, more juggling—less balancing.)*

And by juggling, I also mean all the re-juggling to keep everything moving smoothly in our world.

If you are a working mom, handling business while taking care of a demanding family life, with children and hubby (or no hubby), this book is a tribute to you— and my badge of honor.

Take a bow for your service!

We handle it all. Business, the household, the kids, the day's meals, *and-and-and!* Including all those unforeseen variables. The unknowns that somehow manage to preempt even our finest, meticulously crafted plans. For many of us micro-managers *of life,* this could be a downright killjoy.

So read on, enjoy, feel inspired, and do keep your knees bent at all times—as supermoms we never know which way the wind will blow.

This airing of cautionary wisdom is for you.

INTRODUCTION
—MOVING FORWARD

Welcome to my world. As you read through this book, I imagine parts of it will remind you of your very own world, where chaos is pretty much the going course of any day. If you are a woman who is trying to have, *and manage,* it ALL (family, work, balance), I hear you, girl. Read on.

It's no secret that making it to the flip side of another day is a badge of honor we wear proudly. This book is a tribute to my fellow superwomen, who survive amid all the madness, and have succombed to the reality check that our lives, more often than not—are anything but calm. Yet, we power through, searching for an ounce of fleeting peace. That's where the inner-gold awaits. If we dig deep enough and maintain our focus as we pass through all of the clutter, some of us lucky ones may find a buried self.

In my book, you will see how I divided my daily journey into three sections—bringing relatable sequences into the conversation, such as:

Part 1—Mommy/Wifey Hat

Gets into the start of the day where mornings could be somewhat challenging, throwing even our best laid plans out the window.

I am going to show you what my morning really looks like wearing my Mommy/Wifey hat, and I do mean *really*. From the kids bouncing on the bed as my typical wake-up call, to the struggle to make it out of the house on time, and wearing matching shoes (on good days). From me unavoidably putting my family first, to the fact that breakfast almost always has to happen on the run, even though that's not what I know to be best. I am sharing it all with you, those who I know start their mornings in many of the same ways.

Part 2—Entrepreneur Hat

Taking my next discourse to the middle part of the day, where some of us are on the job or trying to run a business—we take our family tasks with us wherever we go, trying to handle and minimize any family drama from our place of work.

I'm going to lead you through what it's like to wear my Entrepreneur/Businesswoman hat, even though my Mommy/Wifey hat is still firmly planted on my head. I will reveal to you the true, honest way I feel when I get to escape to the office for a moment of peace, and how the guilt of actually getting that escape can really drag me down. You are going to see how chaotic a day in my hectic life can be, how many hats I have to wear (not just individually, but all at the same time). Also, how many times my best-made plans are totally in vain. I am even going to fess up about how I use a special time of the week to slip away and get some *must-have* "me-time" just so I can reset my frazzled nerves. Sound familiar?

Part 3—I'm Home Hat

Wrapping up the day and settling into our evening routine at home is the first chance for us to take a breath and remember why we do it all— for the ones we love. There is no place like home with family. It's the true essence of having it all, empowering us to do it over again the next day.

I will show you the well-hidden side of myself that I rarely disclose. The times when I am wearing my *I'm Home hat*. This hat covers a lot of guilt, whether it's associated with the fast-food dinners I can't seem to avoid or the fact that my children absolutely run the show.

In the end, even with everything—the stress, the guilt, the life of trying to have it all—I am doing my human best. Why would I expose so much of myself? Because I know that through my shared stories of life trials, tribulations, ebbs, and flows, you will see the sweet triumphs along the way. As I trust you will recognize, those sweet triumphs I reveal through my own struggles are not just mine—they are also yours in your own individual journey. And I share with you some of my tips and insights to make your journey just a little smoother.

The following pages are my way of trying to hand you a little bit of sanity ahead of the chaos that is possibly your life, as well. All things considered, you may realize that life of yours is a lot like mine, and these lives we lead are so full—at times they're overwhelming. But being overwhelmed can sometimes mean not just bursting at the seams, but also feeling like our cups are running over with blessings, success, and so much pride in just how much we are capable of achieving.

There is something in this book for every woman. As you read along, it is my greatest hope that you will take from it ample inspiration to feed into your next day of wearing all the hats. Where there's hope for us superwomen, there's a reclaimed sense of ahh. *Of self.*

I AM the woman who has it ALL. Yes, that's me.

Arrogant of me to say? Maybe I should clarify. I have it all because I do it all, and I bet you do too.

You see, something I have discovered along my mom/wife/businesswoman's journey is this: We all have so much in common. We're out here trying to do it all and have it all in this amazing life. We have a family that needs us— kids, husband—while trying to have a successful career, and acting as the glue between the trials and tribulations of our own selves and the people around us who mean the most. The problem is, in spite of so much in common, a lot of us end the day feeling alone in what we face.

As a woman, I find incredible serenity in the fact that I am not on this journey alone. I find camaraderie *everywhere*. It's the lady wrestling two screaming kids away from candy at the grocery store. It's the friend at work making dinner plans with her husband on the phone while typing an email back to a client. It's the mom in the drop-off line at school, hair a mess, not a drop of makeup and still wearing pajama bottoms. I see you, I am you, and we truly are living this life together—this life of trying to have it ALL, because, in reality, *we do.*

We multitasking, multitalented, multifaceted women can find so much solace in each other, but we rarely get a real, authentic look at what goes on behind the makeup, the smiles, and the seemingly full and well-planned lives we lead.

In the reading journey ahead I'm handing you a spyglass into my own hectic life, which is a life I know most of you can relate to all too well. I want you to see because I know when you look closer at me, you will see someone very familiar—*you*.

So, here it goes—this is me—that woman who has everything. This is my journey. And through it, I trust you will find pieces of your own. Take a stroll with me. Let me show you my life, and perhaps reflect some of yours. Along the way, as you follow my stride, I know you will see something profound: the sheer beauty and growth that comes from the chaotic mess that is *our lives* and the incredible experience of having it ALL. *It belongs to us, it's what we signed up for.*

PART 1

Mommy/Wifey Hat

CHAPTER 1

Wake-Up Calls

Most would say their day starts off with a bang. My day, like a lot of modern-day women, starts off with an all-out *explosion*.

Before I even open my eyes, I have two young, bright-eyed children bouncing on my bed. They never fail to remind me that even though the previous day's exhaustion still lingers, it's time to get up, and get going. Somehow, every morning, the not-so-gentle wake-up call from the kids and the long list of To-Dos pull me reluctantly from the embrace of my bed. I get the kids dressed and ready for the day, manage to get breakfast ready for everyone, and even find time to make coffee for myself and my husband.

Most days it's a miracle that I make it out of the house in matching shoes with a face that is even halfway presentable.

I barely have time to choke down my own coffee, let alone think about breakfast for myself, before I dart off to the bedroom to get my own self ready for work. If I'm lucky, I'll know what I'm wearing. If not, my outfit for the day is what I come to first in the closet. My makeup/hair routine gets melded into one haphazard event, and I'm usually already checking emails, dealing with early client calls, and trying to plan my day between lipstick and tracking down my husband's car keys. Seriously, most days it's a miracle that I make it out of the house in matching shoes with a face that is even halfway presentable.

We females are busy people. We're entrepreneurs, professionals, and sometimes family breadwinners. Yet, we're still wives or have significant others who demand our attention/ affection and have children looking to Mom for nearly everything. We cram our days full

4

of responsibilities that demand our attention and our attention alone. To make "having it all" even more stressful, we hold ourselves to these insane standards in how we look, how we mother, and what our relationships should be. We measure success by what others achieve, instead of what we achieve, and then beat ourselves up when we can't do/have/achieve it all.

These incessantly full days lead to incessantly full lives, and maintaining some sense of sanity in the chaos of it all can sound like a fairytale. Trust me when I say I know exactly what that feels like.

I came across a study recently that really put some things into perspective (Pew Research Center / *Six Facts About U.S. Moms*).[1] Highly educated women are having children at higher rates. Even more telling, mothers aren't only spending more time growing their professional lives, but they are also spending more time nurturing their children and bearing the brunt of caregiving responsibilities compared

---

[1] A.W. Geiger, Gretchen Livingston, Kristen Bialik, "6 Facts About U.S. Moms," *Pew Research Center,* May 8, 2019.

to dads. One out of four women are actually doing all this on their own as single mothers. (Amazing!). This goes to show that most of us are in a never-ending daily grind, juggling a ton of responsibilities and commitments, and struggling to find a balance between two worlds: family and business. Another epiphany to be gleaned from the research, many women are *choosing* these really full lives and not just landing there by accident.

Personally, with a family, a home, and a successful business, I find myself having to just power through and swing along with the pendulum (and sometimes madness) of life. I do feel like I have it all, but having it all is one challenging job. And, for us as women, the challenges of balancing work and life can be an overwhelming collaboration of emotional and physical obstacles.

Like most women, after my day gets jump-started by my family, I shift gears toward work to face a new set of responsibilities. All the while, family commitments still flood my thoughts and oftentimes creep into my work-day. In all of this, I am always reminded of one thing: It is me at the center of this hectic life.

In other words, without me, there would be no work-life balance at all, so the balance itself begins with me—*within* me.

So, what do I do? Every morning at some point amid the chaos, I demand a small corner of time for myself. I may shut myself into my office, my car, the bathroom, or pretty much anywhere available that I can be purely alone. I turn off my phone and shut down distractions. Depending on the day, I may have ten minutes or two, but that time, right there, is all mine, and mine alone. In those few quiet moments, I meditate, I pray, I affirm my worthiness, I breathe, and, most importantly, *I rebalance.*

Every morning at some point amid the chaos, I demand a small corner of time for myself.

You see, there is this essential value in starting off one's morning right and *in balance.* Without the balance within yourself, the rest of the day is affected. When your mind, heart, and energy are being pulled in a million directions at any given moment of the day, it's so easy to completely lose focus of your overall goals and even your own self. By the end of the day, you often find that you've given so much to every-one and everything else that there is nothing left for you—the true stabilizer in the storm.

By taking a few quiet moments and call-ing them yours, you get the chance to recenter your thoughts, shrug off some of the stress, and speak a few kind words to yourself to get your day off to a positive start. I get asked a lot by co-workers, friends, and family who recognize just how full my life is, "How do you do it all?" The truth is, my friends, I don't do it all—there are things that simply don't always get done. But I can smile when I say that I do *balance* the whole of everything this wonderful, crazy, amazing, chaotic life has to offer. I think that is one of the biggest keys to living the best life.

If you can totally relate to everything I've just said, then you'll definitely relate to the very fact that we can't get away from the many hats that come with our many job titles—as Mommy, Wifey, CEO, Professional, and Friend—the list goes on for miles. When you have so many roles to fill, how do you keep the family first, through the chaos? How do you manage your professional life without impeding your starring role as the nucleus, and the very facilitator of your family domain? This experience and the acquired insight speak to the maze we all battle to get through every day just so we can get to the other side—of the day. *Then hit REPEAT.*

GIRLFRIEND, you can have it all, but you can't always have it all at the same time. Sometimes you need to pick and choose the priorities of the day.

Chapter Takeaways

- How to start your morning in balance:

    > Before taking on the madness of your day (or whatever you want to call it), it's important to first get *centered* to help stay ahead of, and take on, the day.

    > Try getting up earlier for meditation, yoga or coffee with your dog or cat.

> Practice daily self-affirmations! Affirm your worthiness, your value, and your "I am enough" power every day.

> Step outside of pre-established boundaries, try a new approach, and consider how to approach old challenges from a new direction.

> Journaling can have a soothing effect for *leveling* out your day. Try it. Then go from your innermost thoughts and desires, on the page, and put them into daily practiced action. Why should your best moments of thriving live exclusively inside your journal pages? *This is the point.*

> Make walking or running part of your daily routine. Get ready to feel invigorated by stepping out and forward. Your body will thank you.

> Consider taking an early swim. Another opportunity for you to feel invigorated, where your body also thanks you.

CHAPTER 2

Family First

At the beginning of each day, the deep dive into trying to have it all always begins with my family. I first find that center and balance within myself, so I can be all that and more to those who are the heart and center of my world—my children and my husband. *Family first.* It allows me to keep up with and serve the Mommy/ Wifey role as best as I possibly can for handling what's ahead of any given day. Like many of us women who are trying to have it all, our first and more important role that takes precedence over everything else is to *our families.*

My family is my central focus and affects everything I do.

What does that family-first dynamic look like, trying to have it all? Is it realistic to think as wives, mothers, or partners that we can truly keep our primary focus on the people that matter most, while also having a career? I think we really can. The thing is, to put family first and keep our eye on that prize doesn't just happen—you usually have to fight to keep the family at the center of your world. My family is my central focus and affects everything I do. However, when my family, *literally my world,* is not in balance, then I can't be either.

Consider what happened to me a few weeks ago, as I'm sure most of you can empathize. It was one of *those Mondays*. We had all stayed up a little too late the night before, I was late getting up, and my youngest child woke up with an earache. Amid the chaos, I burned breakfast, forgot to schedule my child's doctor's appointment, and nearly bit my husband's head off when he asked about his keys.

Even though I did make it to work, I seriously could not focus on my list of To-Dos because my family morning did not get off to the right start.

I hear women say this a lot: *Everyone needs so much from me!* Trust me, I can totally relate. I am positive that if I didn't get my children dressed in the morning, their dad would let them out of the house in pajama pants and mismatched socks. If it weren't for me, dear hubby would get drive-thru breakfast (if that) on a daily run because he would spend 20 minutes searching for keys he carelessly left in his pants the day before. I would even go as far as to say that without me, the day wouldn't ever really get started, *at least not on time.* But, just like every other woman, some days I fall short— I have to work to readjust, recenter, and make sure my family knows they are my priority.

That was a bad Monday of mine. The day may have gotten off to a rocky start for all of us, but I couldn't leave it that way. Not only was the rough start bothering me emotionally, but it was also interfering with my productivity at work. The solution, for me, was an early lunch, making the doctor's appointment I'd forgotten, checking in with daycare to make sure my youngest was OKAY, and then surprising my husband at work with his favorite lunch and tons of *sorry-I-was-cranky* affection.

Every Monday morning, no matter what, I have this critical role. It's my job to prepare everyone for the week. We each have our own lives outside of home waiting in the hours ahead in our own separate, yet closely intertwined worlds. And, I am the nucleus, the family facilitator. What I provide for my family Monday morning sets the stage for the rest of the week—I accept that.

Yes, I have a fully mapped out week with my agenda as a professional woman. But, if I don't meet the needs of my children and husband first, I can never fully step into my next role.

There are days that I simply can't be everywhere all at once and the two worlds collide.

Some say that keeping family first is an impossible standard for the business woman to abide by. How can we put family first when we work long hours, have to miss certain milestones, or can't always cook a four-course meal at the end of the day?

I will admit as a woman in a high-powered professional role, the reality is sometimes work has to happen *around* family. There are days that I simply can't be everywhere all at once and the two worlds collide. Sometimes, I make agonizing decisions about how I allocate my time. There are times when I want to be with my children, my husband and simply can't. Just the same, my children and my husband are still my central focus—*always*.

I say putting family first deserves a broader, less judgmental definition more fitting for our modern world. My economical contributions, the fulfillment I hold by doing something I enjoy, the skills I've developed throughout my career—all these things benefit my family in some way or form. My children have a mother they can admire, learn from, and emulate. My husband gets a confident life partner he can respect, working hard alongside him to give our children what they need. Above all, in my eyes, this means my family, is and always will be, *first*.

GIRLFRIEND, tame the guilt monster by asking yourself if whatever you're beating yourself up about will matter in 10 years.

Chapter Takeaways

> Keep the family front and center in your life, but have them contribute and do their part as well.

> Even though we both know you have Supermom powers, give yourself some slack and don't get stuck overloading your morning tasks—ALL on yourself solely. You have options for relieving *that load*—aka, your family. If you don't ask for help, then that load really is all *on you.* There is no point in hoarding your morning tasks all to yourself, where there is absolutely nothing to prove. Your family already knows how amazing you are. Now, you just need to evolve from amazing to smart.

> Drop irrelevant emotional weight and adjust your focus, so your family can help. Remember they are there for you. All you have to do is ask.

> Here is a prime example of sharing your load: Break up your morning routine by allocating some chores to your family. Have them participate wherever they can help to make a difference and take the edge off the start of your day.

CHAPTER 3

Breakfast on the Run

I have a confession to make. Sometimes all of us—my kids, my husband, and me—get fast food for breakfast. There, I said it.

A few days ago, for example, my beloved oldest child decided to let me know about a school project on the morning it was due. To further complicate the morning, the conference I had scheduled had to be moved up 30 minutes, and I'd put off going over my notes the night before. So, I was already cutting things short.

Those days always leave me with this almost unshakeable guilt.

In my haste to feed everybody, because I feel like that's my job, I considered resorting to Lunchables or microwaving a frozen breakfast only to find there was, of course, none. The solution? A quick trip through the Jack in the Box drive-thru with the kids on the way to school. Ideal? No, but at least we all ate something.

Those days always leave me with this almost unshakeable guilt. In my "perfect world" mindset, I would make this hearty, healthy, homemade breakfast every morning. You all know what I mean—crepes from scratch, fresh-squeezed orange juice, eggs cooked to suit, the full chow. I clearly remember breakfast like this when I was a child myself, so that idea is ingrained in me. I do try to achieve a healthy morning meal, but more often than not, we're all so busy scrambling to get out the door that a family breakfast like that sounds more like a pipe dream.

I forgive myself for the shortcoming, but, admittedly, sometimes it's hard. *They* say breakfast is the most important meal of the day. I'm inclined to agree but what about those days when it just can't happen? It's really no wonder something like two-thirds of people don't eat breakfast at all even though most people actually want breakfast. Most of us lead these crazy-busy lives, wearing all these different hats, and the pinnacle point of the day is the morning. However, I must say *they* always have a lot to say about everything. I should try to hold a meeting or form a commission of inquiry with *they* one of these days—when/if I can find them. Anyway, no time to digress. After all, that one precious ever-fleeting part of my day (and daily reality check reminder), where I always come short, is *time*. Which come to think of it, would make the perfect item to add to my shopping list: *time-expanders*. Hope to find it on Amazon.

I have this *Big Life* with kids, a husband, and my business, and I want it all to come together like a well-oiled machine. I want to be the fuel at the center of that machine keeping everyone going, which means I wholeheartedly want to feed my family wholesome healthy meals—especially that important first part of the day.

But at times in my real world, this just doesn't happen, and I know most women can relate. I see other mothers ducking their heads in the drive-thru line and shoving the donut box in the parking lot trash can at work.

A good friend actually called me last week practically ready for a divorce. Much like me, she has kids, a professional career, and a very full life. Her significant other had made an off-handed comment about her not cooking enough—*BIG mistake*. His comment was unthoughtful for sure, but the comment also got drastically amplified because it fueled the guilt she'd already been dealing with as a wife and mother. I saw this in her because that guilt is so familiar to me.

I can make plans to get the day started perfectly, but a lot is beyond my control.

When I pointed out how much I could relate, and that he was a complete jerk for saying it out loud, she calmed down and divorce was off the table by the time we hung up the phone.

Just like my dear friend, I have these intentions to do it all for my family, but it's easy to forget at times that I can't control every variable when I wake up in the morning. No matter how much I want the morning to get started with a nourishing meal delivered by me, my daily life show has three other people included. Because I do share my world with three people who are incredibly dear to me, the room for unforeseen factors is huge. I can make plans to get the day started perfectly, but a lot is beyond my control.

Breakfast is important, sure, but maybe this meal doesn't necessarily have to be perfect or look like what I plan in my mind. Trust me, I fully get that fast food is rarely a healthy choice, and that only adds to the guilt. I have to remind myself what truly matters when I feel that guilt of fast-food breakfast creeping in. When you're juggling a full life like mine, sometimes, all the stars have to align just *so* to be able to cook a complete breakfast every morning. The life I lead as a wife and mother is not the same as the life of my mother before me, or her mother before her. Sometimes, breakfast *on the run* is all that's possible. Some days, *life* happens on the run too. Both are OKAY at the end of the day.

GIRLFRIEND, you need to forgive yourself on the difficult days. Your children are being nurtured and nourished. No one's growth was ever stunted by an Egg McMuffin.

Chapter Takeaways

- Make healthy choices in the *fast-food* lane.

- Quick, do-ahead, healthy breakfast ideas could go something like this:

  > Smoothies or yogurt 'parfaits' (yogurt, fruit, granola) in to-go cups.

  > Egg 'muffins' (omelet ingredients baked in a muffin pan that can be done ahead, then frozen and microwaved in the morning).

  > A banana or apple with a handful of nuts is a nutritionally sound breakfast.

  > Breakfast can be anything! PB&J, grilled cheese, even leftovers (pizza for the win!)

  > Make your husband's favorite lunch to take with him to work before he darts out the door.

  > Prepare sandwiches for your children the night before.

PART 2

Entrepreneur Hat

CHAPTER 4

Escape to the Office

Do you ever need to escape? Let me just say this quickly before I change my mind: *I escape often—okay, I mean a lot.*

As busy as my mornings can be, and stress-inducing as they get because I want the perfect start for everyone, sometimes, finally making it (*err...escaping*) to my office is a welcome sigh of relief.

Maybe my office doesn't sound like much of an escape. This is where my professional day gets started after all—I still have a business to run, a million things demanding my attention.

But in the middle of disengaging from the daily morning chaos with my family and preparing to dive into the workday at hand, I have this quiet, inner-sanctum, my "me-space," where I can usually catch my breath.

Do I ever feel ashamed that some days I look forward to the inner-sanctum, the stillness of my office before office hours or after hours? Absolutely.

Full disclosure, there are days when I still desperately need an *escape*—even if the reality of that escape is just a few quiet moments, alone, and in my office. Case in point, when COVID-19 entered the scene in 2020 and forced most of my team to work from home, my office was down to a skeleton staff. I opted to go to the office because attempting to work from home, in the midst of my daily family dynamic, would have been next to impossible.

Do I ever feel ashamed that some days I look forward to the inner-sanctum, the stillness of my office before office hours or after hours? Absolutely. Does it change the fact that I continue to look forward to that some days? Absolutely not. Nevertheless, the irony of it all is no matter how much I view my morning office as my escape, I never truly escape. I don't really think that's possible.

I'll give you a good example of what I mean.

The nature of my professional life might mean including a press interview, proposals, presentations, and negotiations, as my business continues to grow in the public sphere. I don't mind these added items to my day, but they do require a certain level of peace and focus. Last Friday, after an especially exhausting week, I happened to have one of those interviews scheduled via Skype to discuss the success of my business. This particular interview was scheduled to happen way too early in the morning—no doubt, not the best time for me. But it was the only time slot available for me and the interviewer.

Now, technically, I could have *dressed from the waist up* and done the interview in the comfort of my home that morning. But, instead,

I chose to rush off to my office. I needed to do this interview in peace without the almost-guaranteed disruptions of my children and hubby still in the house. After the trying week I'd had, I also wanted to command that bit of time to focus solely on my work. I left boxed cereal and milk on the table and then stole away to get myself prepared, leaving my husband to deal with everything between the morning routine of searching for forever-lost small shoes, to the dutiful drop-off of our kids at school. He barely got a cheek-kiss before I slipped out the door, and, yes, I felt a little guilty, but still a little giddy, about my escape.

The interview once I got to my office went well enough, but it really is a wonder I made it through. From the moment I sat down at my desk, nearly my entire focus was consumed by the fact that I'd promised my kids French toast the night before, likely left something on in the kitchen, and didn't even bother to tell my husband I loved him before I rushed out the door.

Those afterthoughts of an especially hectic morning at home always follow me to work no matter how much I view getting to the office as an escape. Those thoughts stream through my consciousness like a broken record. They're the nagging guilt every working mother/wife/professional knows too well:

- *Fast-food breakfast, again—what kind of mother am I?*

- *Why didn't I show my babies more attention before leaving them?*

- *Good grief—I shouldn't have been so short with my husband!*

- *Maybe I should've . . .*

- *I probably shouldn't have . . .*

- *Why didn't I . . .*

- *Why can't I . . .*

This negative rhetoric is not healthy. Trust me, I know, but I'm just as guilty of it at times as any other woman.

I'd be willing to bet you have a similar story. As women, we have all these demands and expectations placed on us or even chosen by us thanks to our best intentions to meet the day-to-day needs of our families.

If we can do all these things and still be *wives, mothers, partners, and friends,* I think that speaks volumes about us women.

Yet, we still step out into our own professional roles and, to be honest, I think we're pretty much killin' it!

A colleague and I were discussing something recently that really made me think. The number of female CEOs of Fortune 500 companies continues to reach record highs year after year. Plus, hard-working women are starting to dominate everything from engineering to law, many even outperforming and outranking their male counterparts. If we can do all these things and still be *wives, mothers, partners, and friends,* I think that speaks volumes about us women.

Maybe sometimes we need to escape—to the office, to the spa, to our own bathrooms with the door locked. With all we manage, I feel like we deserve these little moments we can claim as ours, no matter how small they may be.

GIRLFRIEND, needing to escape to work doesn't mean you love your family any less. And no one ever criticized a man for separating home and family in order to be professional.

Chapter Takeaways

- There is nothing wrong with needing to focus on your work. Consider the benefits:

  > Virginia Woolf wrote that a woman needs "a room of one's own." Timeless wisdom.

  > The more you do at work, and stick with it, the more you can help to provide for your family. Keeping the job is essential!

  > Your co-workers appreciate you more because you are "in the zone" and keeping your eye on the task of the moment.

  > The sooner you can finish at work, the sooner you can get to other items of your daily To-Do List.

- Recognize the value of creating an escape spot in and out of your home.

  > Reclaim an unused spot (stair landing, basement, walk-in closet, etc.)

  > Sign up for a room at the library (it's free and includes WIFI!)

  > Make the most of outdoor space at your work and watch how nature can affect reviving the senses, as well as recharging your energy.

  > Practice persistence in what you aspire to, such as *stubbornness with a purpose.*

CHAPTER 5

Guilt-Ridden at Work

I. Feel. Guilty. Three little words that have far more power than anyone realizes, including me.

I have got to let you all in on something because this is something that needs to be said: Every morning, once I make my grand escape to my office, ready for a productive day, I can't stop thinking about all the pending tasks related to my family. And I can't stop feeling *guilty*.

Even in the inner-sanctum of my office, where I sometimes long to be just for some peace and quiet away from the day-to-day drama at home, my mind goes there— *to the guilt*. Those three beings that demand oh-so-much from me, my two kiddos and my hubby, and though they make me all-out crazy at times, they are very much lodged at the forefront of my mind. Being at my office does not change that—as they are right there with me at work, too. *Every. Single. Day.*

That nagging guilt is something I like to call *Mommy/Wifey Guilt Syndrome.*

As a business professional, I have clients, staff members, and major business matters to handle, but out of the blue, the entirety of my day is filled with moments of beating myself up. I have learned something, too. It never really matters what happened that morning, what kind of breakfast I made or didn't, or how much love I gave to my children or husband. I can never shake those thoughts and feelings that I did not do enough.

That nagging guilt is something I like to call *Mommy/Wifey Guilt Syndrome.* I have even given the disorder a fancy acronym: MWGS. Sound familiar? Welcome to my world.

Most of the time, a little guilt is a good thing. Really, feeling guilty just means you have a healthy conscience as a wife and a mother. After all, it is guilt that reminds you to be better, to do better. BUT the funny thing about guilt is there is this fine line between healthy, necessary feelings of inadequacy and disruptive, unhealthy guilt, or MWGS.

MWGS can be so bad that everything can trigger feelings of guilt. Personally, I know my triggers, and they are kind of hard to avoid *most days:*

- Coworker/girlfriend/female relative gushes about one-on-one time with her partner (something I struggle to make happen).

- Someone mentions something posi-tive about mothering their own children (doesn't even have to be anything grand).

- Girlfriend/female relative seems to have all these great holidays/vacation trips happen-ing *(when I can barely schedule the vacation to Mexico my kid won at school).*

- When I realize I have forgotten something, anything (it literally could be forgetting to tie a shoe. NOT joking).

These little things and more can send me into
an all-out MWGS fit. Then I can't focus and all
I can see is where I am lacking. I know this is
not healthy, and I also know there is probably
not a mother alive who loves her family that
has not experienced MWGS on some level.

I recall reading an enlightening piece on
Mom Guilt in *Psychology Today* by Marika
Lindholm, PhD.[1] The article really did hit a lot
of points I could relate to—but one thing, in
particular, stuck out to me: *"You can't parent
powerfully from guilt."* In other words, if you
are constantly dealing with guilt, you are un-
dermining your own ability to be a powerful
mother.

Let's ponder about this for a second to gain
more perspective.

A while back, for about two straight weeks
work was demanding so much of my time that
I had very little time with my children. When
I say little time, I mean just an hour or two a
few nights a week, or not seeing them at all,

---

[1] Marika Lindholm, Ph.D, "Don't Let 'Mom Guilt' Make
You a Worse Parent," *Psychology Today,* February 22,
2019.

including in the morning. Now, normally (Mom Guilt speaking here and feeling the need to clarify to thwart judgment), I have a relatively strict rule for myself. Time off from work is literally *OFF* time from work—which means during my time at home in the afternoon or on a day off, I make all efforts to be wholly present for my children and husband. However, at this point in time, some dire business needs were consuming an extensive amount of my time and energy, so yes, work followed me home.

Don't judge—you know you've been there.

Because I was barely able to be present, my Mommy/Wifey guilt was at an all-time high. I'm talking *kids-could-ask-for-a-pony-and-I'd-say-yes, hubby-could ask-for-a-new-flat-screen-TV-and-I'd-say-yes* HIGH. Don't judge—you know you've been there. Anyway, my oldest child decided one night that he wanted ice cream at bedtime. It was a firm, *NO*, at first. I know what happens when he eats junk before bed, and it was already beyond bedtime. Of course, that night, he let me know I was the worst mother ever because his best friend gets to eat ice cream at bedtime *all the time*—with sprinkles, no less.

My child was obviously doing what he could to get his way, but my guilty self almost immediately caved. I was exhausted, my children were being neglected (okay, not really), and I was already feeling like the worst mom ever (even without my son's help). So, I hand-delivered that vanilla ice cream—with sprinkles and a smile—and watched him gobble it all down, with his face telling me he was amazed he had gotten his way.

1:00 a.m.—"Mooommmy, my belly huuurts . . ."

2:00 a.m.—Regurgitated vanilla ice cream—and sprinkles—EVERYWHERE.

5:00 a.m.—Three loads of laundry in, a half-asleep child getting bathed for the fourth time, my morning alarm goes off.

This is what happens when you let go of your mothering power and let guilt parent for you. I knew better, but let guilt guide me *anyway*. Lesson learned.

The thing I have learned in all my struggles with Mommy/Wifey guilt—*the syndrome that won't go away*—is yes, guilt's unavoidable, but, no, we can't let guilt dictate life.

A good friend once told me, "The worst guilt is to accept an unearned guilt." *Point taken.*

That spoke volumes to me. If we women are doing the absolute best we can do to balance work/mom/wife responsibilities, where is there really guilt to accept? Aren't we just carrying a burden we didn't earn by doing something wrong? I have to remind myself, daily, that I can't be the best me in any of my roles if I'm running around letting guilt run the show. I've done nothing to earn that guilt, and my guess is, neither have you.

GIRLFRIEND, don't let guilt dictate your life. Would you blame your sister or your best friend the way you blame yourself?

Chapter Takeaways

- The Guilt Monster revisited.

  > Stop doing it ALL for others. Remember yourself and your needs as well.

  > You deserve whatever you desire. That's right. Keep telling yourself that—*until you TRULY believe it.*

  > Don't feed into your guilt. You have better things to do with your valuable time.

CHAPTER 6

Daily Family Multi-Tasking

Ever heard of a full plate? That pretty much describes a day in my life—just pick any day. *They're all full!* In fact, most days, I'm juggling not just my own, but the plates of those who are in my inner-circle as well. Yes, that would be my family, and all their individual plates—literally stockpiled, collectively, on top of mine. It's a wonder I don't drop something. All things considered, I'm afraid that day is just around the corner. *Look out below!*

Every morning, despite being at my office handling the day-to-day affairs of my business,

I've actually merged all these incessant hats into *one*, because I realize they *all* never really leave my head.

I am still *Mommy*, as much as I am still *Wifey*, and I handle those duties right along with everything else—as the multiple hats I wear might call for at any given moment of the day. That, besides the neon *"Help me!"* sign glazed across my forehead (with frown lines on the house). After all, and who's counting, but I don't have a bunch of hats in my proverbial closet for no reason—just like most women. Like most of us girls, I wear all my hats *at once.* That's right. I've actually merged all these incessant hats into *one,* because I realize they *all* never really leave my head. *It's my "Call Me a Hero" hat.* Therein lies the superhero part of my day. *You're welcome.*

I wear this hat at all times, even at the office. My business needs me but my nearest and dearest (aka, my family) need logistics, planning, and a multi-tasking handler to keep everything moving along smoothly—*in their worlds.* This is my role to play, and I would love to say I accept it with grace, and while most days I think I do, things however really do get tough.

My day starts super early with hungry kids, a list of To-Dos, and a husband who truly needs my help to get his own day started. Once I'm at the office, which sometimes happens late because of at-home responsibilities, my workday is not just filled with work, clients, and business matters. Oh no, it goes well beyond. *I'm also . . .*

- Making appointments for the kids or husband.

- Planning dinner with my husband, simply trying to be the adult while working his culinary desires into our schedule.

- Calculating how to leave work early so I can pick up the kids from school.

Beyond work and school, I am *also* my kiddos' designated chauffeur in the afternoon for all their extracurricular activities—swimming, martial arts classes, piano lessons. These are just the day-to-day, multi-tasking duties that at times have me stretched in more directions than manageable, in spite of all my advance planning and effort—*to stay ahead of the circus.* Then there are those unforeseen *variables* to consider.

You know, the out-of-the blue stuff that is be-yond our control, and just happens to broadside our day—somehow magically thrown into an al-ready chaotic mix with a cry of, *"Help me!"*

I have always considered myself a planner. I make lists. My phone practically doubles as a daily planner, and yes, post-it notes are my jam—if not my way of life. But here's the thing about making plans when you are a wife/mom/entrepreneur: It's those gosh-darn *variables* (aka, the unknowns) that somehow creep into our day—and like most creeps, I just want them to go away. They are a busy woman's nemesis when it comes to her best-laid plans.

If you have a business, a husband, and chil-dren, you are constantly juggling, constantly adjusting, constantly *handling* all those some-times-dramatic variables. In other words, keep your knees bent at all times, as us girls never know which way the wind is going to blow until we actually deep dive into our day.

At any given moment, the day I so meticulously planned can be preempted, as it is suddenly pulled in every new direction imaginable, thanks to the many people who rely on me.

Some days, I'm not even sure why I bother to plan, because almost anything goes and almost anything is sure to happen—it's back to those gosh-darn variables. You all know the variables as well as me, I'm sure. It's the:

"Babe, I can't find my keys,"—in the morning, when I am already running late.

"Mommy, I'm sick—can you pick me up from school?"—midday, when I am in the middle of a meeting.

"Hey, this client needs your help,"—at quitting time, when I am supposed to pick up my kids from school or some extra-curricular activity.

Now, let me interject here. I have a luxury most women don't. As a business owner, my work hours are set by me, but I am still responsible for keeping the business afloat and growing. Plus, my demanding clients are like my *other* children. So, regardless of the schedule I make for myself, I can't neglect my duties—they are all important, professionally and personally, and play into each other as part of my daily balancing/juggling act. *(Okay, more juggling—less balancing).*

With all that being said, I'm not just juggling all those full plates on a daily basis, I'm also *re-juggling* those plates so everything keeps moving smoothly.

If you have never taken a look at American Time Use Surveys[1] published by the U.S. Bureau of Labor Statistics, the information can be quite an eye-opening. Women spend almost double the time as men on daily household activities and caring for household members. We also spend more time shopping, handling food preparation, and managing the household. Women are also more likely, than men, to hold more than one job at one time[2]—and go to college *while also* holding a job. None of us are alone as we dash around wearing our superhero hats, carrying full plates, and dealing with frazzled nerves— lest we not forget those (yes, the nerves, un-hinged et al). Just part of our package deal for making it ALL work!

---

[1] Editorial Staff, "Average Minutes per Day Men and Women Spent in Household Activities," *U.S. Bureau of Labor Statistics,* December 20, 2016.

[2] Editorial Staff, "Women in the Labor Force," *U.S. Bureau of Labor Statistics,* December 2019.

No, we ladies with full plates don't wear capes at all— we have our special (hard) hats— *and you best believe those Hero hats sparkle.*

There's this phrase I like: *Not all superheroes wear capes.* No, we ladies with full plates don't wear capes at all—we have our special (hard) hats—*and you best believe those Hero hats sparkle.* Every day, we open our eyes, pull on our "Call Me a Hero" hats, and pick up those plates full of maneuvering everyday life. After all, what is life, *every day,* without trying to maneuver some facet of it—be it our family or professional existence. We may even have a plan, but we also know we can go from our so-called plan to zero in seconds, thanks to about-face situations that are far beyond our control. *Back to those unforeseen variables again.* The unknowns that somehow manage to preempt even our finest, meticulously crafted plans. For many of us micro-managers *of life,* this could be a downright killjoy.

At the end of the day, no matter how much of a chaotic mess that day may have been,

I was the handler, and I handled it—like a big girl, as I am expected to. Just like you, I handled the business, the husband, the clients, the kids, the supper, and even the *drama du jour*—because we all know each day is never short of that.

So yes, while things get messy for us heroes/handlers, giving our all for family and business, doing our humanly possible best—and despite being in the thick of all that madness, we still manage to walk away with our full plates still in the air, our special hats dazzling, *and our cups completely running over.*

GIRLFRIEND, reward your own heroics and recognize your star Super Woman powers sometime take a village of supporters who are there for you.

Chapter Takeaways

> Give yourself a reality check and ask whether your plate is simply too full to truly handle by yourself. Distribute any overload you don't have to do by yourself.

> Ask for help when you need it—and even when you don't need it. Be realistic with yourself. Supermoms, this means you.

> Enough with those runaway To-Do lists. Or worse, the lists of the lists of the lists, of the lists of more lists. Yes, you're amazing. But apart from that self-affirmation, what you are not is a machine. And if you try to go there, even remotely (into the machine-verse), then don't be surprised to have a machine adverse effect. And short-circuiting yourself is certainly no fun.

> Before adding anything else on that list *(any of your lists, just pick one),* think of those around you who could possibly help pinch-hit through the day—and take some of that heavy-lifting off your Superwoman shoulders. You don't have to do it ALL. *You really don't.*

> Do practice the power of flexibility. And we're talking about going well beyond your early morning yoga stretches. This flexibility has more to do with stretching your daily field of possibilities. It starts by not being so hard or rigid on yourself. Allow yourself the space, and the reality check, to recognize you are still only human—despite all your superpowers.

> Every opportunity you have, don't forget to share your load with others. The ones who care, from family to friends, will hear you and help. There is not much to figure out here—but to recognize you are not alone. And if you do try to do it all on your own, you will have only yourself to blame.

CHAPTER 7

Martial Arts Me-Time

I **L-O-V-E** martial arts. *I know, I know*—I probably don't look like the type. Kung-fu, judo, karate—it's one of the best things since sliced bread. You'd never guess, right?

OKAY, so maybe I'm not in the dojo myself karate-chopping boards and practicing roundhouse kicks, although that would be an interesting sight. But I still LOVE martial arts just the same. Here's why: My young sons happen to be totally into their martial arts class.

You may be a little jealous right about now of my incredible love of watching my sons during their session, but before this gets too sidetracked, let me explain. Martial arts sessions take a nice little while, like a long enough while to have my own escape from my daily chaos. While I wait for my sons to finish these sessions, I have my own martial arts me-time. *A pre-planned, well-deserved, always-overdue meet-up with my girlfriend and sometimes an adjustment at the chiropractor's office.* Can you relate?

But these girl-time visits serve as a makeshift means of escaping the chaos of the daily grind.

Every week, my girlfriend and I use this 'martial arts me-time' to escape the daily chaos, share our woes, vent our frustrations, and catch up since the week before. Some days, we even enjoy a late-afternoon drink. We talk, we laugh, we complain, and we both know exactly why we need this little carved-out time slot for just ourselves.

Technically, I could go straight home and wait there, just as she could skip the meet-up and spend more time with her family. But these girl-time visits serve as a makeshift means of escaping the chaos of the daily grind. And, you know what, it's all-out therapeutic. This right here, our brief girl-time visit, has become especially valuable to both of us. Just like me, my bestie has a lot on her plate—including her own family circus waiting at home.

While we sit and commiserate, as besties generally do, we're doing more than getting away—we're recharging our internal strength so we can suck it up and dive right back into our very full lives. We both step away refreshed, nerves soothed, and feeling just a bit lighter so we can tackle the rest of the week.

Of course, when our little escape is over, I'm right back into my day and my own full life. I pick up my sons from their martial arts session and head home. I never quite know what I might be walking into when I get there with my hubby waiting for me. I shudder to think, the house could be in utter disarray. Yet, somehow, that doesn't bother me all that much on *those evenings*. My little me-time escape was essentially my reset, my refresh button, and I'm ready for whatever.

Just as an overworked machine gets all bogged down when it's stuck on repeat, so do us women with our ever-full plates. We get bogged down, physically and emotionally. We lose sleep, we overwork, we sacrifice every minute we have for those we love. We stretch ourselves so thin to achieve goals, meet expectations, and take care of everyone else, and we eventually reach a point when we are completely drained.

We all too easily forget that if we don't take care of ourselves first, everyone around us pays the price.

Recently, I read an interesting post on *Psychology Today,* which my girlfriend and I discussed in-depth during our last escape.[1] Let me tell you, we were really feeling this discussion. Studies show that women feel more confident, independent, and satisfied in life with a career or a job. BUT, working women are also more likely to struggle when it comes

---

[1] Geeta Ramakrishnan, "Dear Working Woman, Don't Forget Your Psychological Well-Being," *Psychology Today,* November 27, 2019

to striking a balance with their emotional well-being. *Why?*

It probably won't come as a surprise that the threat to our emotional well-being lies in the pressure of juggling multiple responsibilities. We wear all these hats, every day, but we fail to ever take our hats off and just be, just relax.

Some of us get stressed out, emotional, and anxious, and instead of stopping and just breathing, we keep pushing harder, continuing to drown ourselves in all of our responsibilities. We all too easily forget that if we don't take care of ourselves first, everyone around us pays the price.

My dear hubby, and he truly is dear, once questioned my weekly escape. He never pushed the issue, and I believe he was truly just curious as to why those few hours I carved out during the week were so important to me. *As that Mommy/Wifey guilt crept in just because he asked.* I skipped my me-time escape that week. And you know what? I was edgy, snappy with everyone in the house, and even more exhausted before the week was out. By the weekend, my hubby was begging me to go somewhere and just take a breather. It's so nice when a significant other can recognize the value of that must-have escape time for their damsel in distress.

Now, at least once a week, like clockwork, I get to leave work early and take my precious children to their beloved martial arts class. I get—*no, I TAKE*—my own little martial arts me-time escape with great I-deserve-this latitude. Trust me when I say, I get just as much out of my little escape as my young sons gets at the dojo, possibly even more.

Have you escaped lately?

GIRLFRIEND, we all need an opportunity to recharge. Adult relationships that allow us to vent are an important part of our support system—allowing us to release stress.

Chapter Takeaways

> Even though taking a break is probably not in your daily realm of possibilities (not for this working mom, right?), still if you could try to stretch what is really doable in your day, you should definitely consider the benefits of taking a break—as highlighted in *The Wellbeing Thesis / The Importance of Taking Breaks.*[1] It's that or something's got to give. So, make it work in your favor.

> The thing about sending your kids to martial arts so you could have some me-time, well, *news flash*—you don't have to send them anywhere. Maybe you can have a trusted friend or family member take the kids off your hands for a short period in the day, while you can go do *YOU* in whichever way will help to feed your senses and give you the alone me-time you crave.

> Practice daily moments of solitude and mental clarity so you can focus on what's important: *your vision of a fulfilling life that takes care of your family.*

---

1 "The Importance of Taking Breaks," The Wellbeing Thesis.

> Find a quiet place to collect your thoughts and eliminate emotional clutter. Sometimes you have to steal these moments for yourself, but do TAKE them—these moments can be a prelude toward true growth and finding contentment within yourself.

PART 3

I'm Home Hat

CHAPTER 8

Fast Food Dinner Guilt

Sometimes, I'm just out of steam—there's not much energy left for home cooking. On those occasions, sometimes more than I care to admit, fast food has become an easy go-to after work. *Ladies, can you relate?* Just think of those can't-beat positives: No planning, no required energy, and no messy kitchen. I'm all in for this convenience! Just an easy pick-up and go, feed the fam, and end the day. *McDonald's, Burger King, In-N-Out . . .* we visit them all.

The ease of fast food is undeniably attractive, even when I know it's not the best option. After work, picking up my two sons from school, plus running around for extracurricular activities, a quick detour to the closest fast-food stop is the most convenient way to tackle dinner for everyone in one fell swoop. *And done!* Of course, this quick-and-easy option is never without the trademark Mommy/Wifey guilt. I always feel like I could have, should have, done more—and by more, I mean making a healthy dinner at home in spite of being completely spent running on fumes from an already exhaustive day.

The fast-tracking of our lives, *between work and home,* is part of our daily fabric.

Considering today's fast-paced culture *(aka, microwave society)* is all about giving and getting most things fast and easy, fast food is no exception. We are moving faster than we ever have and accomplishing more than we ever thought possible. Let's wrap our heads around this reality check. The fast-tracking of our lives, *between work and home,* is part of our daily fabric. Albeit the only way to make it all work is with a few cut corners and not without some level of cost or sacrifice.

For example, the modern family gets approximately 38 minutes of quality, together time on any given weekday (according to Her / This is the Average Amount of "Quality Time" a Modern Family Spends Together on Weekdays).[1] Imagine that—a measly 38 minutes. Gives me shudders! Doesn't our family deserve more? While the answer is a profound YES for any good caring wife and mother, there is still no getting around the limited amount of time available to spend with our family members. It is actually the lack of free time for us all-over-the-map women that makes even our best intentions a non-starter. In a perfect world scenario, my first choice would be to always prepare nourishing home-cooked meals for my family. However, in my very real world, where most days go sideways with *something* beyond my control—I am left opting for fast food as that's all my ever-fleeting day will allow.

------

[1] Megan Cassidy, "This is the Average Amount of 'Quality Time' a Modern Family Spends Together on Weekdays," *Her*.

I'm not living in the dark. I know full-well, fast food is usually lacking *quality*. Fact. When it comes to grabbing dinner on the run, it's a bit of a double-edged sword. While I may be trying to make room for more quality time, I may also be sacrificing quality nourishment for my family. And still, I can't help but make my way to the nearest drive-thru in haste to feed my family, especially after having a busy day at work. Guiltless dinner just doesn't have space on the day's menu because yours truly chef/mommy/wifey/hero is *exhausted—despite all my best intentions to do an about-face on fast food.* I've grown accustomed to fast-food dinner guilt, and I even have my habitual justifications for these self-contradicting actions ready to go *as needed.* Quite a treadmill I've gotten myself onto, with no simple way of getting off in sight.

For the busy woman with a full life and accompanying mega schedule, capable of breaking the best of us—alas the *give-and-take* of our days leaves us with less give, and more take.

Many days my option is to either feed my family fast or sacrifice whatever time and energy I have left to pull something together at home. The *quick and easy* Plan B always comes with guilt, when there is no more juice left in me for making the initial home-cooked Plan A happen. Hence, the unavoidable fast-food guilt due to sacrificing quality when it comes to what's best for my family. Some weeks are pretty bad, *like fast-food-every-night bad.* How do I internally justify it, allow myself a pass, to prevent being eaten up by guilt? I simply make well-intentioned mental notes that next week will be better. Next week, I will make more time. Next week, I will create a meal plan and do some meal prep. Next week, I will cook every night. *Next week . . .*

Once again, I make a promise to myself that next week I will definitely do better— *and mean it.*

In the moment, these justifications make me feel better. Sometimes I can even let go of the guilt entirely. But when the new week rolls in, I often get stuck on the repeat fast-food-dinner circuit—with the same old guilt of the week before, *all over again.* So, the aspired next-week approach has become another missed opportunity, *somehow circumvented by day-to-day life. An ongoing week-to-week reoccurrence, or so it seems.*

Once again, I make a promise to myself that next week I will definitely do better—*and mean it.* This is a subconscious inner-dance that seems to make everything okay for this *on-the-Go-Go-Go* woman. Though in reality, that better week may never actually happen. And so, the clash of guilt/justification keeps right on going. It's like I'm running on a treadmill that I control, but I'm still at odds with my own self at all times—which definitely has a contrary effect on that control.

The thing is, I feel like this incessant dance is part of what makes me a good wife/mother, just like it makes you a good wife/mother. Sounds crazy, right? But check this out . . . The whole process doesn't just apply to fast food. Consider this: Any working mother will tell you they go to bed thinking, *"Tomorrow, I'll do better."*

It's the days when you spend too much time at work, forget to give your hubby the time of day, simply don't have time, lose patience, yell too much, don't exercise, eat horribly. *Sound familiar?* You know the drill. This guilt/justification internal clash is just a sign that we always feel our potential to do more for our families and our lives—even if that *more* is a *home-cooked dinner.*

Maybe some weeks I feed my family fast food for dinner every night for a week straight. Maybe I beat myself up, rationalize, and justify. Maybe you do too. *But you know what?* We're all still doing great in this life, and we all know full well we can step it up because otherwise, we wouldn't challenge ourselves to do just that. So yes, fast-food guilt is very real. Worry over the quality of our partnering skills is even more real. In the end, we keep trying to power through against all odds—*a perfectly okay, possibly even healthy, sign of our true abilities.*

GIRLFRIEND, let go of dinner guilt and focus on what really counts—your children are safe, fed and loved.

Chapter Takeaways

- Consider these tips for quick and easy dinners:

    > Make ahead and freeze meals.

    > Throw-together dinners using sheet pans, instant pots or slow cookers.

    > Throw-together dinners made by combining premade ingredients.

- Okay, so you picked up fast food for dinner. If your kids can get over it, while devouring their dinners, so should you.

CHAPTER 9

The Children Run the Show

Shhh!—don't you dare tell my boys, but they absolutely run the show at my house and in my life. I like to act like I'm the boss, but that's really just a facade. On the outside, things look convincing. But the credible reality is, our boys may be the youngest souls in the house, though they truly do dictate everything. And I do mean everything.

Take yesterday, for example:

- I had to set my alarm an hour early; my oldest needed help with a last-minute project before school.

- I got to the office 30 minutes late; my youngest son had a meltdown over a toy on the way to school.

- Lunch—picked up what one of the boys needed for an afterschool activity.

- Made the boys' dentist/doctor appointments between client calls yesterday afternoon.

- Left work mid-afternoon for about an unplanned hour; my oldest *just then* realized the project we got up early to finish was still at home.

- Rescheduled my own doctor's appointment for yesterday afternoon; had to play catch up at work and stay a bit later with such a hectic day.

- Associates made plans to get together for drinks on Friday—I passed; Friday was promised to the kids for pizza/camping movie night.

Let's face it, my children quite literally run my life. Yours probably do too—it's just how motherhood works. Plain fact: a mother's day is never quite done (even if technically yes, it is done at bedtime, but still *no* on a whole other level). I trust your day probably looks a lot like mine.

You know, the kind of stuff we can't plan for—that just happens *anyway.*

Every daily endeavor of my life is planned, arranged, and organized around them, *the children,* first and foremost. Even when it doesn't start that way, it ends that way. My husband is also a main priority, of course, but the children always take precedence in my daily routine because they *need* so much of me and my time. They preempt every task on my To-Do List. Those little boys determine what hours I keep at the office, my day-to-day appointments (both professional and personal), and even what time I open and close my eyes for the day. *Sound familiar?* Welcome to my world— uh, the daily awakening of our shared mutual world if you are a working mother. Nothing comes closer to that truth among us moms— where day-to-day anything goes and anything can happen. You know, the kind of stuff we can't plan for—that just happens *anyway.*

I bet you can relate. Most mothers can, even though speaking what I just said out loud in front of our kids would be a big mistake. Those adorable kids of ours, if they really knew how much control they have: let's just say it would be disastrous. Horns would sprout, we would see sharp teeth we knew nothing about, and trying to control them would be implausible. *They. Can. Never. Know.*

From morning to night, every aspect of everything I do facilitates the needs of my children. I'm more than OKAY with that—raising children to be eventual adults is the most important job ever. Sometimes, the idea of that is overwhelming to consider, especially when, as parents, we tend to get about 30 minutes of time for ourselves on a daily basis (according to the *New York Post / Parents Get Way Less Than an Hour per Day of 'Me-Time').*[1] Let's think about that, when there's time of course.

When my head hits the pillow at night, *I'm out.* Exhausted. But the next morning, I WILL begin again as the entrepreneurial woman, the wife, and the mother who pushes beyond feasible limits to make sure my kids are good at the end of the day.

---

[1] Tyler Schmall, *"Parents Get Way Less Than an Hour per Day of 'Me-Time,'"* New York Post, October 3, 2018.

In the middle of all of this, even when putting my children first and foremost, I make mistakes and sacrifice what I know to be *best* for what I know to be *easy*. I've made peace with this over time—no mom ever does all things completely perfect for her children. I've also come to know that most moms never measure up to their own standards in their minds. I believe when we realize this to be true, our jobs become a little easier. Maybe it relieves mothers from some of that undue pressure we feel on a daily basis.

I'm constantly juggling all of my plates on any given day—*seriously, pick a day, literally just any day*—and I'm always juggling something with hopefully not too many "look out below" moments; that would be a good day. I strive to make sure my children are happy and healthy, even though sometimes my good-parenting attempts go right out the window for those pleading little faces.

Those babies are still my world, they still run my show, and they still go to sleep at night with a mommy who did her best for that day.

What mother can't relate? Sometimes (and for some of us, maybe all of the time), our kids want things not in their best interest, like eating too many sweets or staying up *way* past their bedtime. I know you get me when I say sometimes I cave when they simply plead with me. My "Power of No" is completely shot. But you know what? Those babies are still my world, they still run my show, and they still go to sleep at night with a mommy who did her best for that day. On some nights, they go to sleep with a mommy who may be better the next day. *Both* involve my children ending the day with a mother who loves them dearly.

While my days may be all over the map, my world nonetheless runs around my children, every day. After all, they are the precious souls at the epicenter of everything I do. I will never have a more important job than being a mother, and putting them first is easy because they complete my universe.

My world, *my sense of purpose,* would not be the same without them pulling on my heart-strings and leading the show that is *my life.*

If they only knew what power they hold in the palms of their sticky, sweet little hands. But, hey mommy sisters—let's just keep that between us.

GIRLFRIEND, don't let the perfect be the enemy of the good. Children don't need perfect parents—they need good parents who put their needs before their parents' wants.

Chapter Takeaways

- Here are some tips for keeping kids' schedules sane:

  > Make a chart to keep your children and yourself on track for day-to-day activities.

  > Be realistic about what is truly doable on your To-Do List. In other words, don't overload list(s) with undoable tasks.

  > Have your husband pitch in with daily tasks as well.

- Learn how to recognize the important things.

- Keep your attention on the long-term plan for your children.

- Give your vision, your goals, and your priorities unwavering attention.

CHAPTER 10

Life Goes On

What do you think about before you fall asleep? I've always wondered this about other people. I remember hearing somewhere once that what's on your mind before you fall asleep tells you a lot about who you are as a person. Maybe I believe that, and maybe I don't, but I do know one thing for certain. As my exhausted head rests on my pillow at night, just before I drift off to sleep, I think: *This is life. My fabulous life.*

I don't have those thoughts with any level of dismay or disdain. The thing is, no matter how tough my day was, how many hoops and hurdles I jumped through and over, or how exhausted

I may be, I signed up for this life. From getting married to running a business to making a family—I did this. And right at present, in the here-and-now of my life's evolution, I am grateful to be precisely where I am. *In my life.*

From the kids to the hubby to the business—this life of mine took shape and took flight. *My life.*

When you think about it, life starts out for most of us like a ball of clay—no real shape or plan but so many possibilities. That was me at the beginning of my young adult life, with all the trials and tribulations that lay before me. I never knew which way the wind would blow or how my choices would mold me. Nevertheless, every time the opportunity presented itself, I went all in with one big leap of faith and gave my best to everything. From the kids to the hubby to the business—this life of mine took shape and took flight. *My life.*

Some aspects of life challenge me, and some aspects feel like they were graciously provided for me. My husband, for example, is my rock. He gives his unrelenting support, his never-ending devotion as the father of our children and my ever-loving husband. Without question, my course has been smoothed by his presence through everything this life involves: raising the children, growing my thriving business, multi-tasking between work and the kids, with all the extracurricular activities flanked into our days. His steps alongside mine give this life more meaning and ease. *This is our life of our making.*

While this path of mine may not always be easy, with oftentimes more ebbs than flows, there is a comfort in the ritualistic chaos that has become part of the fabric of my life. Sometimes, that's exactly how I like to view my life: like a fabric tapestry filled with unique experiential threads. This fabric is woven with sweat equity, it's incredibly full and overwhelmingly rich with experience—colorful as it is indelible. I truly wouldn't change anything—other than possibly more time to enjoy it. Every threaded moment, the struggles, even the pivotal *OMG* and *WHAT-NOW?* moments, have made this tapestry of life stronger, and more beautiful, for the experience—including all those curveball moments (that never ceased to remind us of why they're called "curveballs"). *This amazing ride of a life has made me who I am.*

Above everything, this life of mine has made me resilient. And on those impossible days, nothing short of fierce—which has gotten me to the other side, *of those days.* The challenges, unexpected twists, and anything-goes days are constantly proving just how strong I am. This mighty force, all in this human frame, is the embodiment of all the potential I truly hold. I am my own reminder and self-revealing surprise, of not only what I am capable of, but what I can handle. *Back to my fierce self.* Ladies, can you feel me?

Some mornings I'm a mess, wondering how I'll make it all come together. And some nights, I may be totally wiped out, completely drained. Yet, despite the challenges between sunrise and sundown (sometimes, too many to count though most are easily recounted), here I am: still standing and cherishing every last experience. After all, every piece, every moment, every thread is managed for the sake of building and maintaining the life and family I have right now. *It's the:*

- Insane mornings of getting everyone ready, fed, and out the door.

- Incessant plate juggling between work and the daily needs and affairs of my family.

- Unexpected, blind-siding moments that force me to be as flexible as the wind.

- Stress of closing out the day—taking care of dinner, homework, and bedtime.

- Emotional whiplash of jumping between feeling not good enough and overwhelmingly blessed.

We are committed, we are fierce, and as we power through (all our "full of it" days), we remain resilient.

Just like every other woman in my shoes, some days I feel inadequate, ill-prepared, and lacking. Some days I make big mistakes, most days I sacrifice my time for someone else, and every day I face some new *challenge-de-jour*. And on some special days, I am astonished at

just how much I have managed to achieve—
all that went into a 24-hour stretch of my life.

We mothers/wives/businesswomen are
superheroes. To do it ALL, no question about
it. Even more noteworthy, our superhero
capes and true powers are well hidden behind
our stoic "I'm-OKAY" smiles—with sometimes
haphazardly applied makeup, and feelings of
lack that keep our modesty in check. We face
unimaginable challenges, and yet we over-
come and persevere. We are committed, we
are fierce, and as we power through (all our
"full of it" days), we remain resilient. And
some of us are *invincible,* as we continue
to run our world around the worlds of our
people—our families—in spite of what gets
thrown at our feet. *I trust we could swap stories on those gems.*

We do all we can to make sure their lives are
happy and complete, and in the process, *our
lives* are happy and complete as well. That's
where the magic is, when it all *somehow* comes
full circle. The life of our making, from where
it started (that ball of clay), to where our journey continues to take shape.

In the big scheme of things, despite the hurdles of my daily efforts, I am constantly reminded that this is a test—if not a testament—of my strength and my will. All wrapped up in one *aha,* "I'm fighting harder" badge of honor to make all my worlds work. And even when it seems against all odds, *life goes on.* Yes! I will make it to the flip side of another day, no matter how challenging. My superhero wings are spread in their fierce-flyer best and *I've totally got this!*

How are your wings holding up? If I've got fly, then I'm willing to bet you've got fly as well—to soar for days. Ladies, it's in me and it's in all of us to power our course forward. No matter how complicated and intense it may be. I got this. We all got this. *My life. Your life.* With all that makes it what it is today. The good, the not-so-good, and all the magic in between that sees us through our journey. Trust in the process. After all, life as we know it—an ongoing daily discovery about ourselves and what we are truly capable of—is and always has been, *only a test.* You know, the kind where the only way to score and move forward is to simply show up for the new day that awaits what you will make of it. *Copy that!*

GIRLFRIEND, take the time to enjoy and be grateful for the life you have. Children grow up too fast and the parenting journey will be over before you realize it.

Chapter Takeaways

> The benefits of practicing gratitude can go a long way.

> Try journaling all you appreciate, now, and for the future.

> Check in with your sisters and girlfriends.

> Problems sometime look much smaller from a fresh perspective. For example, if you struggle to overcome self-doubt, taking on a totally new project or learning a new skill may help.

> It's much easier to get where you want to be when you have a clear view of where you're going at all times.

> If something in your life has no place in your long-term vision, let it go.

> Prioritize and plan your next day according to what's most important. Get ahead of the potential circus of the new day.

> Remember, good days become good weeks, good months, and great years.

> Your day, your family, your life, ALL OF IT, starts and ends with you—where you are constantly being reminded of your true power. Even if it's in the form of being tested, taking on a new challenge can turn into an opportunity. *You got this girl!*

THE AUTHORS

ABY LILIAN MAMBOLEO, JD/MBA has come a long way since her native Nairobi, Kenya, youth. A self-made American businesswoman and a role model living her motto-driven course, "I'm a B.I.T." (Billionaire in Training), she is the founder of the publishing imprint, Mamboleo Media Group.

In her new book, *The Key to Guilt-Free Success for Working Moms,* Mamboleo channels her acquired wisdom as a working wife and mother. She is also the co-author of *Business Life & the Universe, Volume 6,* which is a No. 1 Amazon bestseller. She has additionally co-authored *The Entrepreneur's Funding Guide: 100 Places to Get Over $100K to Fund Your Business.*

Achieving her success through service and heart, Mamboleo is a recognized consultant and thought leader. She has further taught business owners innovative ways to manage, grow and scale their business.

Having honed her skills as an advisor in the recruiting industry, Mamboleo is also the owner and president of International Outsourcing. She had previously co-founded and built a parent company that was sold to a publicly traded organization.

TANY SOUSSANA is a public relations professional based in Los Angeles where she runs her company, The Soussana Group/TSGpr, in tandem with her bespoke content development service, epiContent. Before her start-up, she was associated with the prestigious public relations firm, Rogers & Cowan, where she became the founding director of the Literary Unit as a result of her successful campaign for the diet book and cult fitness phenomenon, *The Zone*—which catapulted to a No. 1 *New York Times* bestseller for more than 50 consecutive weeks.

Prior to her entrée into books, Soussana also worked in the firm's celebrity and film divisions, and became a lead writer for the chairman. She was involved with multiple Hollywood campaigns for A-list luminaries. Her niche work in entertainment and publishing has dovetailed into concentrated written works, where she enjoys making a creative contribution.

Lightning Source UK Ltd.
Milton Keynes UK
UKHW011955020123
414739UK00019B/200